THE BRASS SERPENT

by **Eric A. Kimmel**
Illustrated by Joanna Miller

PITSPOPANY

NEW YORK ◇ JERUSALEM

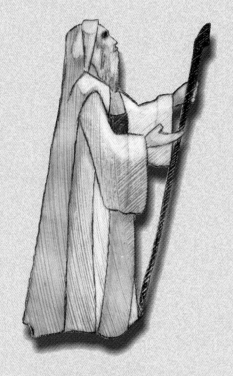

THE BRASS SERPENT

Published by Pitspopany Press
Text Copyright © 2002 by Eric A. Kimmel
Illustrations Copyright © 2002 by Joanna Miller

Cover Design: Benjie Herskowitz

Cloth ISBN: 1-930143-41-9
Paper ISBN: 1-930143-42-7

Pitspopany Press titles may be purchased for fund raising programs by schools and organizations by contacting:
Marketing Director, Pitspopany Press
40 East 78th Street, Suite 16D, New York, New York 10021
Tel: (800) 232-2931
Fax: (212) 472-6253
Email: pitspop@netvision.net.il
Web Site: www.pitspopany.com

Printed in Israel

To Emma

Eric Kimmel

_____

These illustrations are dedicated to five individuals who, without their support along the way, none of this would have been possible:

To my beautiful mother and sister.

To my friend and mentor, Alex Bostic.

To my son and inspiration, Mordechai Yehoshua.

To my partner and husband, Yitzchok, who has always helped me believe that anything is possible.

Joanna Miller

Also by Eric A. Kimmel

WHY THE SNAKE CRAWLS ON ITS BELLY

"The germ of this story is taken from an ancient Rabbinic source which will fascinate anyone who has read the account of Adam and Eve in the Bible and wondered: Why – of all the punishments possible – was the snake punished with the loss of his legs. This story is also one of hope for the characters in the biblical saga, and for all mankind."

Eric Kimmel

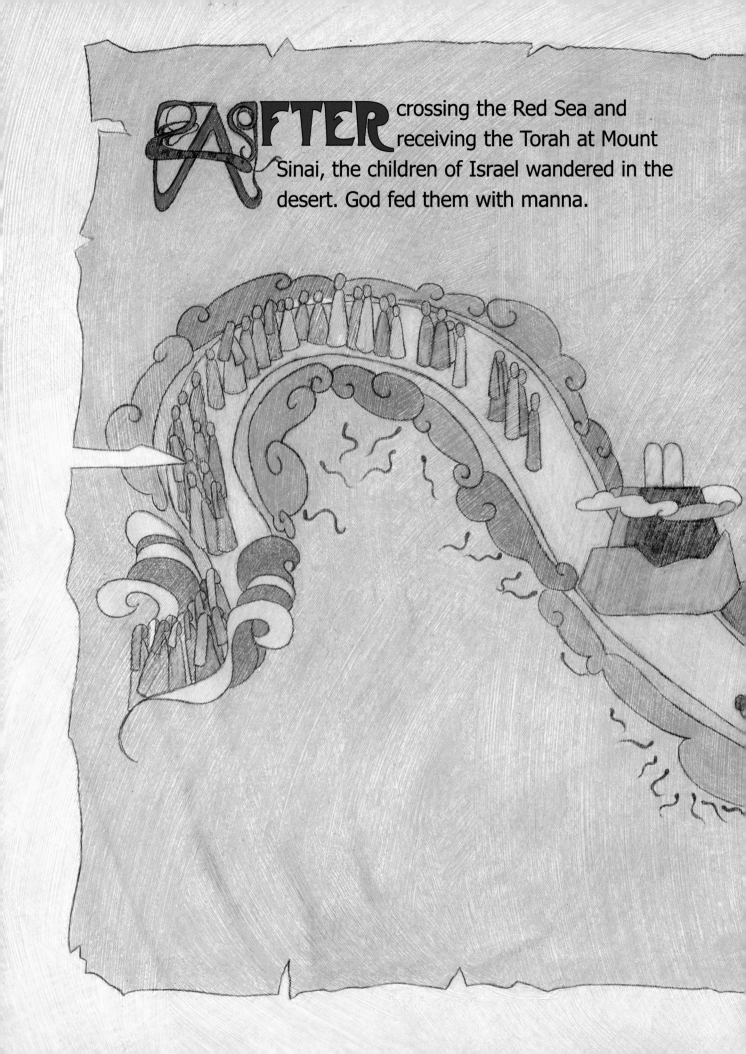

AFTER crossing the Red Sea and receiving the Torah at Mount Sinai, the children of Israel wandered in the desert. God fed them with manna.

He gave them water to drink from Miriam's Well, which followed the Israelites on their journey to the Promised Land.

The desert was a terrifying place, filled with poisonous snakes. These snakes traveled for miles to attack anyone who entered their territory. God protected the Israelites from the snakes. He covered their camp with His Cloud of Glory. The snakes could not penetrate the shining wall of light. Those who tried were burned to ashes.

The snakes vowed to destroy Israel. They followed the tribes through the sand. They told themselves, "One day the Israelites will make God angry. He will withdraw the Holy Cloud. Then we will rush in and destroy them!"

God led the children of Israel to the land of Edom, which they would have to cross to enter Promised Land. The wind carried the fragrance of Canaan.

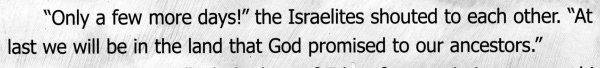

"Only a few more days!" the Israelites shouted to each other. "At last we will be in the land that God promised to our ancestors."

God told Moses, "Ask the king of Edom for permission to cross his land. The Edomites are the children of Esav, your forefather Jacob's brother. They are your cousins. Let there not be war between you."

But the king of Edom refused to allow the Israelites to cross his land. "If your people cross my land," he told Moses, "they will drink all the water. They will devour the food. Your animals will eat the grass. Nothing will remain for my people."

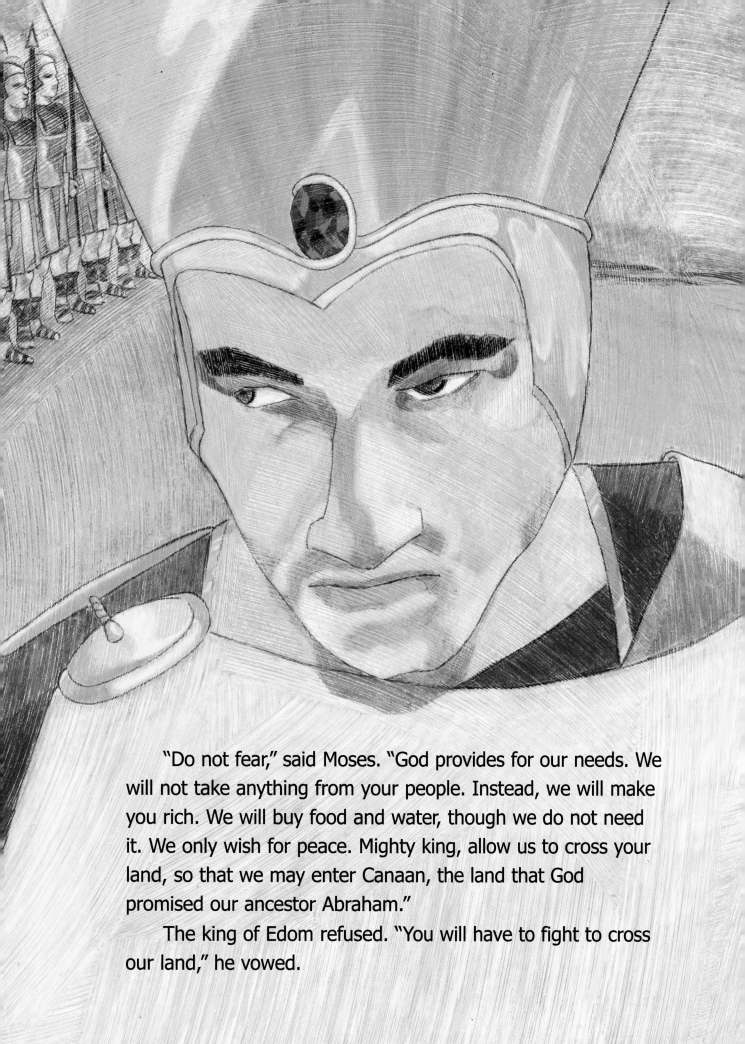

"Do not fear," said Moses. "God provides for our needs. We will not take anything from your people. Instead, we will make you rich. We will buy food and water, though we do not need it. We only wish for peace. Mighty king, allow us to cross your land, so that we may enter Canaan, the land that God promised our ancestor Abraham."

The king of Edom refused. "You will have to fight to cross our land," he vowed.

"Then fight we will," Moses answered.

"Nothing will keep us out of Canaan."

But God said to Moses, "The children of Jacob and Esav must not shed each other's blood. If the Edomites will not let you cross, you must go another way."

The Israelites grew angry when Moses told them what God wanted. "Are we to be frightened by a few Edomites? God will stand with us. We will slaughter our enemies. Not one will be left alive."

Moses tried to reason with the people. "We cannot disobey God. God feeds us and protects us. Trust in Him. He will bring us to Canaan in His own time."

"Moses is our leader," some of the Israelites said. "We must do what he asks."

However, most were too angry to listen. "We want to enter Canaan now! If God will not bring us there, we will go there ourselves!"

The Israelites prepared for battle.

God said to Moses, "Do these people think they can enter the Promised Land without Me? They have forgotten all the good I have done. I will have to remind them."

God suddenly lifted the Cloud of Glory from their camp. The Israelites no longer felt God's presence in their midst. With the Cloud of Glory gone, there was nothing to prevent the snakes from attacking them.

"Ssssseeeee! God has forssssssaken the Israelites!" The snakes slithered into the camp, biting everyone in reach.

The children of Israel screamed in agony. Only Moses and those who listened to his words were not bitten. Beams of glory shined from Moses' face. The snakes feared to approach him.

Those bitten cried to Moses. "Help us! Ask God to forgive us! We are sorry we disobeyed! Do not let us perish!"

"Holy One, have mercy on your people!" Moses prayed. "Do not let them die in the desert."

God answered Moses' prayer. "I will forgive them for your sake. I will not let them die."

God told Moses to make a brass serpent. As soon as it was finished, it coiled on the ground at Moses' feet. God's power had brought it to life, though it was made of metal.

The serpent coiled around Moses' staff. "Raise me up," it said. "Let the people see me."

Moses raised his staff. "Look up!" he called to the Israelites. "God has sent this brass snake as a sign of forgiveness. Know that the God who created these snakes will also save you from them. Do not lose hope. Raise your eyes to heaven. God is watching. Ask God for mercy. He will help you!"

These words came too late for many. They had lost hope. They ceased to believe in God or Moses. They refused to look at the snake. And they died.

But others, with their last breath, heeded Moses' words. They looked at the brass serpent, then raised their eyes higher, toward heaven. They still believed in God and in the words of Moses, His prophet.

God turned His face toward the children of Israel. The Cloud of Glory descended, driving out the snakes and their poison, healing the people. God had saved the Israelites once more.

Moses placed the brass serpent near the Ark that contained the Ten Commandments and other holy objects. "God has the power to turn away trouble and suffering," Moses reminded the Israelites. "Through God's power, the snake that harms becomes the snake that heals."

The brass serpent remained near the Ark, shedding its skin every year. The priests saved the snake's brass scales in a special jar, for they were holy objects. When King Solomon built the Temple in Jerusalem, he used these shining scales to cover the Temple's doors. The gates of the Temple shined like the sun on the heights above Jerusalem.

Today, you can still see the brass serpent coiled around Moses' staff when you visit the doctor's office. The image of the serpent on the doctor's wall reminds us to raise our eyes to heaven whenever we are sick and need God's help.

It reminds us to trust in God, Who heals, loves, and protects all who believe in Him.